3 Look at the number words and what they mean. What do you notice about each word?

6 - six   6th - sixth

Word	Meaning
sextuple	six times as much
hexagon	a flat shape with six equal sides
sextuplets	six children born at the same time
sextet	six singers or musicians

1	2	3	4	5	6	7	8	9	10
11	12	13	14	15	16	17	18	19	20
21	22	23	24	25	26	27	28	29	30
31	32	33	34	35	36	37	38	39	40
41	42	43	44	45	46	47	48	49	50
51	52	53	54	55	56	57	58	59	60
61	62	63	64	65	66	67	68	69	70
71	72	73	74	75	76	77	78	79	80
81	82	83	84	85	86	87	88	89	90
91	92	93	94	95	96	97	98	99	100

The numbers in green show the six times table. What is the pattern of the numbers in the green squares?

17

4 What pattern can you see on the number grid?

Published by Ladybird Books Ltd
A Penguin Company
Penguin Books Ltd, 80 Strand, London WC2R 0RL, UK
Penguin Books Australia Ltd, Camberwell, Victoria, Australia
Penguin Books (NZ) Ltd, Cnr Airbourne and Rosedale Roads, Albany, Auckland, 1310, New Zealand

5 7 9 10 8 6 4

Printed in Italy

Times Tables for School

Illustrated by John Cunliffe

Ladybird

1 Times Table

0 x 1 = 0
1 x 1 = 1
2 x 1 = 2
3 x 1 = 3
4 x 1 = 4
5 x 1 = 5
6 x 1 = 6
7 x 1 = 7
8 x 1 = 8
9 x 1 = 9
10 x 1 = 10
11 x 1 = 11
12 x 1 = 12

1 - one 1st - first

Word	**Meaning**
single	one, on its own
unicycle	one-wheeled cycle
solo	for one person
once	one time

1	2	3	4	5	6	7	8	9	10
11	12	13	14	15	16	17	18	19	20
21	22	23	24	25	26	27	28	29	30
31	32	33	34	35	36	37	38	39	40
41	42	43	44	45	46	47	48	49	50
51	52	53	54	55	56	57	58	59	60
61	62	63	64	65	66	67	68	69	70
71	72	73	74	75	76	77	78	79	80
81	82	83	84	85	86	87	88	89	90
91	92	93	94	95	96	97	98	99	100

Here are the numbers from one to one
hundred in a number grid. This shows the
one times table.

2 Times Table

How many fish can we catch?

$$0 \times 2 = 0$$
$$1 \times 2 = 2$$
$$2 \times 2 = 4$$
$$3 \times 2 = 6$$
$$4 \times 2 = 8$$
$$5 \times 2 = 10$$
$$6 \times 2 = 12$$
$$7 \times 2 = 14$$
$$8 \times 2 = 16$$
$$9 \times 2 = 18$$
$$10 \times 2 = 20$$
$$11 \times 2 = 22$$
$$12 \times 2 = 24$$

2 - two   2nd - second

Word	Meaning
double	two times as much
pair	two matching items
bicycle	two-wheeled cycle
twice	two times
twins	two children born at the same time

1	2	3	4	5	6	7	8	9	10
11	12	13	14	15	16	17	18	19	20
21	22	23	24	25	26	27	28	29	30
31	32	33	34	35	36	37	38	39	40
41	42	43	44	45	46	47	48	49	50
51	52	53	54	55	56	57	58	59	60
61	62	63	64	65	66	67	68	69	70
71	72	73	74	75	76	77	78	79	80
81	82	83	84	85	86	87	88	89	90
91	92	93	94	95	96	97	98	99	100

The numbers in blue show the pattern of the
two times table. What do you notice about the
numbers in the blue columns?

9

3 Times Table

0 x 3 = 0
1 x 3 = 3
2 x 3 = 6
3 x 3 = 9
4 x 3 = 12
5 x 3 = 15
6 x 3 = 18
7 x 3 = 21
8 x 3 = 24
9 x 3 = 27
10 x 3 = 30
11 x 3 = 33
12 x 3 = 36

How many mice are eating cheese?

3 - three   3rd - third

Word	Meaning
triple, treble	three times as much
tricycle	three-wheeled cycle
triangle	three-sided flat shape
trilogy	three part book, play or film
triplets	three children born at the same time

1	2	3	4	5	6	7	8	9	10
11	12	13	14	15	16	17	18	19	20
21	22	23	24	25	26	27	28	29	30
31	32	33	34	35	36	37	38	39	40
41	42	43	44	45	46	47	48	49	50
51	52	53	54	55	56	57	58	59	60
61	62	63	64	65	66	67	68	69	70
71	72	73	74	75	76	77	78	79	80
81	82	83	84	85	86	87	88	89	90
91	92	93	94	95	96	97	98	99	100

The numbers in red show the pattern of the three times table. What do you notice about the red numbers going downwards?

4 Times Table

$$0 \times 4 = 0$$
$$1 \times 4 = 4$$
$$2 \times 4 = 8$$
$$3 \times 4 = 12$$
$$4 \times 4 = 16$$
$$5 \times 4 = 20$$
$$6 \times 4 = 24$$
$$7 \times 4 = 28$$
$$8 \times 4 = 32$$
$$9 \times 4 = 36$$
$$10 \times 4 = 40$$
$$11 \times 4 = 44$$
$$12 \times 4 = 48$$

How many sides does my kite have?

4 - four   4th - fourth

Word	Meaning
quadruple	four times as much
quarter	one of four equal parts of a whole
square	a flat shape with four equal sides
quadruplets	four children born at the same time

1	2	3	4	5	6	7	8	9	10
11	12	13	14	15	16	17	18	19	20
21	22	23	24	25	26	27	28	29	30
31	32	33	34	35	36	37	38	39	40
41	42	43	44	45	46	47	48	49	50
51	52	53	54	55	56	57	58	59	60
61	62	63	64	65	66	67	68	69	70
71	72	73	74	75	76	77	78	79	80
81	82	83	84	85	86	87	88	89	90
91	92	93	94	95	96	97	98	99	100

The numbers in orange show the four times table. What do you notice about it?
Does it remind you of the two times table?

5 Times Table

0 x 5 = 0
1 x 5 = 5
2 x 5 = 10
3 x 5 = 15
4 x 5 = 20
5 x 5 = 25
6 x 5 = 30
7 x 5 = 35
8 x 5 = 40
9 x 5 = 45
10 x 5 = 50
11 x 5 = 55
12 x 5 = 60

How many stars are in the sky?

5 - five   5th - fifth

Word	Meaning
quintuple	five times as much
pentagon	a shape with five sides
quintet	five singers or musicians
pentathlon	an athletics contest with five events

1	2	3	4	5	6	7	8	9	10
11	12	13	14	15	16	17	18	19	20
21	22	23	24	25	26	27	28	29	30
31	32	33	34	35	36	37	38	39	40
41	42	43	44	45	46	47	48	49	50
51	52	53	54	55	56	57	58	59	60
61	62	63	64	65	66	67	68	69	70
71	72	73	74	75	76	77	78	79	80
81	82	83	84	85	86	87	88	89	90
91	92	93	94	95	96	97	98	99	100

The numbers in yellow show the five times table.
Look at the yellow columns. Do you notice
anything about the units?

6 Times Table

0 x 6 = 0
1 x 6 = 6
2 x 6 = 12
3 x 6 = 18
4 x 6 = 24
5 x 6 = 30
6 x 6 = 36
7 x 6 = 42
8 x 6 = 48
9 x 6 = 54
10 x 6 = 60
11 x 6 = 66
12 x 6 = 72

How many spots does each butterfly have?

6 - six   6th - sixth

Word	Meaning
sextuple	six times as much
hexagon	a flat shape with six equal sides
sextuplets	six children born at the same time
sextet	six singers or musicians

1	2	3	4	5	6	7	8	9	10
11	12	13	14	15	16	17	18	19	20
21	22	23	24	25	26	27	28	29	30
31	32	33	34	35	36	37	38	39	40
41	42	43	44	45	46	47	48	49	50
51	52	53	54	55	56	57	58	59	60
61	62	63	64	65	66	67	68	69	70
71	72	73	74	75	76	77	78	79	80
81	82	83	84	85	86	87	88	89	90
91	92	93	94	95	96	97	98	99	100

The numbers in green show the six times table. What is the pattern of the numbers in the green squares?

7 Times Table

0 x 7 =   0
1 x 7 =   7
2 x 7 = 14
3 x 7 = 21
4 x 7 = 28
5 x 7 = 35
6 x 7 = 42
7 x 7 = 49
8 x 7 = 56
9 x 7 = 63
10 x 7 = 70
11 x 7 = 77
12 x 7 = 84

How many colours are in the rainbow?

7 - seven   7th - seventh

Word	Meaning
September	in Roman times, this was the seventh month of the year
septennial	lasting for seven years
heptagon	a seven-sided flat shape
septet	seven singers or musicians

1	2	3	4	5	6	7	8	9	10
11	12	13	14	15	16	17	18	19	20
21	22	23	24	25	26	27	28	29	30
31	32	33	34	35	36	37	38	39	40
41	42	43	44	45	46	47	48	49	50
51	52	53	54	55	56	57	58	59	60
61	62	63	64	65	66	67	68	69	70
71	72	73	74	75	76	77	78	79	80
81	82	83	84	85	86	87	88	89	90
91	92	93	94	95	96	97	98	99	100

The numbers in yellow show the pattern of the seven times table. What do you notice this time?

8 Times Table

0 x 8 =   0
1 x 8 =   8
2 x 8 = 16
3 x 8 = 24
4 x 8 = 32
5 x 8 = 40
6 x 8 = 48
7 x 8 = 56
8 x 8 = 64
9 x 8 = 72
10 x 8 = 80
11 x 8 = 88
12 x 8 = 96

How many legs does an octopus have?

8 - eight   8th - eighth

Word	Meaning
October	in Roman times, this was the eighth month of the year
octagon	an eight-sided flat shape
octopus	a sea creature with eight tentacles
octet	eight singers or musicians

1	2	3	4	5	6	7	8	9	10
11	12	13	14	15	16	17	18	19	20
21	22	23	24	25	26	27	28	29	30
31	32	33	34	35	36	37	38	39	40
41	42	43	44	45	46	47	48	49	50
51	52	53	54	55	56	57	58	59	60
61	62	63	64	65	66	67	68	69	70
71	72	73	74	75	76	77	78	79	80
81	82	83	84	85	86	87	88	89	90
91	92	93	94	95	96	97	98	99	100

The numbers in blue show the pattern of the eight times table. Can you see a pattern in the numbers below the blue squares?

9 Times Table

0 x 9 = 0
1 x 9 = 9
2 x 9 = 18
3 x 9 = 27
4 x 9 = 36
5 x 9 = 45
6 x 9 = 54
7 x 9 = 63
8 x 9 = 72
9 x 9 = 81
10 x 9 = 90
11 x 9 = 99
12 x 9 = 108

9 - nine   9th - ninth

Word	Meaning
November	in Roman times, this was the ninth month of the year
nonagon	nine-sided flat shape
nonet	nine singers or musicians

1	2	3	4	5	6	7	8	9	10
11	12	13	14	15	16	17	18	19	20
21	22	23	24	25	26	27	28	29	30
31	32	33	34	35	36	37	38	39	40
41	42	43	44	45	46	47	48	49	50
51	52	53	54	55	56	57	58	59	60
61	62	63	64	65	66	67	68	69	70
71	72	73	74	75	76	77	78	79	80
81	82	83	84	85	86	87	88	89	90
91	92	93	94	95	96	97	98	99	100

The numbers in pink show the pattern of the nine times table. What is the pattern of the tens? What is the pattern of the units?

10 Times Table

0 x 10 =   0
1 x 10 = 10
2 x 10 = 20
3 x 10 = 30
4 x 10 = 40
5 x 10 = 50
6 x 10 = 60
7 x 10 = 70
8 x 10 = 80
9 x 10 = 90
10 x 10 = 100
11 x 10 = 110
12 x 10 = 120

How many skittles are in the alley?

10 - ten 10th - tenth

Word	Meaning
December	in Roman times, this was the tenth month
decade	ten years
decagon	ten-sided shape
decathlon	an athletic contest with ten events

1	2	3	4	5	6	7	8	9	10
11	12	13	14	15	16	17	18	19	20
21	22	23	24	25	26	27	28	29	30
31	32	33	34	35	36	37	38	39	40
41	42	43	44	45	46	47	48	49	50
51	52	53	54	55	56	57	58	59	60
61	62	63	64	65	66	67	68	69	70
71	72	73	74	75	76	77	78	79	80
81	82	83	84	85	86	87	88	89	90
91	92	93	94	95	96	97	98	99	100

The numbers in blue show the ten times table.
What is the pattern of the tens?
What is the pattern of the units?

11 Times Table

0 x 11 =   0
1 x 11 =   11
2 x 11 =   22
3 x 11 =   33
4 x 11 =   44
5 x 11 =   55
6 x 11 =   66
7 x 11 =   77
8 x 11 =   88
9 x 11 =   99
10 x 11 = 110
11 x 11 = 121
12 x 11 = 132

How many apples are there?

11- eleven 11th - eleventh

Word

hendecagon

Meaning

eleven-sided flat shape

1	2	3	4	5	6	7	8	9	10
11	12	13	14	15	16	17	18	19	20
21	22	23	24	25	26	27	28	29	30
31	32	33	34	35	36	37	38	39	40
41	42	43	44	45	46	47	48	49	50
51	52	53	54	55	56	57	58	59	60
61	62	63	64	65	66	67	68	69	70
71	72	73	74	75	76	77	78	79	80
81	82	83	84	85	86	87	88	89	90
91	92	93	94	95	96	97	98	99	100

The numbers in green show the eleven times table.
What do you notice about the tens and units?
Can you see a link with the one times table?

12 Times Table

0 x 12 = 0
1 x 12 = 12
2 x 12 = 24
3 x 12 = 36
4 x 12 = 48
5 x 12 = 60
6 x 12 = 72
7 x 12 = 84
8 x 12 = 96
9 x 12 = 108
10 x 12 = 120
11 x 12 = 132
12 x 12 = 144

How many balls am I juggling?

12 - twelve 12th - twelfth

Word   **Meaning**

dodecagon   twelve-sided flat shape

dozen   twelve of something

1	2	3	4	5	6	7	8	9	10
11	12	13	14	15	16	17	18	19	20
21	22	23	24	25	26	27	28	29	30
31	32	33	34	35	36	37	38	39	40
41	42	43	44	45	46	47	48	49	50
51	52	53	54	55	56	57	58	59	60
61	62	63	64	65	66	67	68	69	70
71	72	73	74	75	76	77	78	79	80
81	82	83	84	85	86	87	88	89	90
91	92	93	94	95	96	97	98	99	100

The numbers in purple show the twelve times table. What is the pattern of the numbers this time?

29

1 Times Table	2 Times Table	3 Times Table
0 x 1 = 0	0 x 2 = 0	0 x 3 = 0
1 x 1 = 1	1 x 2 = 2	1 x 3 = 3
2 x 1 = 2	2 x 2 = 4	2 x 3 = 6
3 x 1 = 3	3 x 2 = 6	3 x 3 = 9
4 x 1 = 4	4 x 2 = 8	4 x 3 = 12
5 x 1 = 5	5 x 2 = 10	5 x 3 = 15
6 x 1 = 6	6 x 2 = 12	6 x 3 = 18
7 x 1 = 7	7 x 2 = 14	7 x 3 = 21
8 x 1 = 8	8 x 2 = 16	8 x 3 = 24
9 x 1 = 9	9 x 2 = 18	9 x 3 = 27
10 x 1 = 10	10 x 2 = 20	10 x 3 = 30
11 x 1 = 11	11 x 2 = 22	11 x 3 = 33
12 x 1 = 12	12 x 2 = 24	12 x 3 = 36

7 Times Table	8 Times Table	9 Times Table
0 x 7 = 0	0 x 8 = 0	0 x 9 = 0
1 x 7 = 7	1 x 8 = 8	1 x 9 = 9
2 x 7 = 14	2 x 8 = 16	2 x 9 = 18
3 x 7 = 21	3 x 8 = 24	3 x 9 = 27
4 x 7 = 28	4 x 8 = 32	4 x 9 = 36
5 x 7 = 35	5 x 8 = 40	5 x 9 = 45
6 x 7 = 42	6 x 8 = 48	6 x 9 = 54
7 x 7 = 49	7 x 8 = 56	7 x 9 = 63
8 x 7 = 56	8 x 8 = 64	8 x 9 = 72
9 x 7 = 63	9 x 8 = 72	9 x 9 = 81
10 x 7 = 70	10 x 8 = 80	10 x 9 = 90
11 x 7 = 77	11 x 8 = 88	11 x 9 = 99
12 x 7 = 84	12 x 8 = 96	12 x 9 = 108